MoneyWords™

MoneyWords™

Easy-to-Use Copywriting & Marketing Secrets That Sell Anything to Anyone

Designed by Sean Edwards
EdwardsPublishingHouse.com

Cover Design by Juan Lopez Design
JuanLopezDesign.net

Published in Spokane, Washington, by Ray Edwards International, Inc.

Ray Edwards International, Inc.
2910 E 57th Ave
Suite 5 #330
Spokane, WA 99223

RayEdwards.com

ISBN-13: 978-1500990749
ISBN-10: 1500990744

Table of Contents

About the Author

His sales copy is amazingly effective — having sold an estimated $100 million in products and services.

Ray's all-star list of clients includes New York Times best-selling authors Tony Robbins, Jack Canfield, and Mark Victor Hansen (creators of *Chicken Soup for the Soul*), Joel Comm (author of *Twitter Power, Ka-Ching,* and *The Adsense Code*), Robert Allen (author of *Nothing Down* and *Creating Wealth*), and Ra ymond Aaron (author of *Double Your Income Doing What You Love*).

Ray has written thousands of pages of copy–radio commercials, TV commercials, direct mail pieces, one-sheets, fliers, brochures, billboards, music-on-hold scripts, training manuals, corporate policy and procedures, web site copy, and email marketing campaigns.

He speaks frequently at seminars on copywriting, promotions, and marketing for professionals in those fields.

He has appeared in magazines, newspapers, trade journals, and on national radio and TV.

Ray is the author of the #1 best-seller *Writing Riches*.

For more resources, a weekly Internet radio show (podcast), and to subscribe to Ray's FREE email newsletter, visit RayEdwards.com

What They Say About Ray

"He is generous with his teachings and holds nothing back."
– **Joel Comm, New York Times best-selling author of *Twitter Power*, *Ka-Ching*, and *The Adsense Code***

"He is simply one of the best living copywriters today."
- **Mike Filsaime**

"Ray has written sales copy for some of the top Internet marketers, as well as other businesses... and not just one-time gigs... his clients come back to do business with him again and again. Why would they do that? Only one reason... because what he does gets results."
- **Martin Howey, Owner, TopLine Business Solutions**

"Ray Edwards is the master of direct response copywriting. The results of my working with him have literally catapulted me into the million dollar revenue makers in the direct response marketing industry."
- **Jack Bosch, Orbit Investments**

"Highest integrity, a pleasure to work with... and fantastic work. I love working with Ray."
- **Jeff Walker, Creator of *Product Launch Formula***

FREE Audio Seminar:

Copywriting Quickstart

Claim Your FREE Audio Seminar and Bonuses ...

- The *Copywriting Quickstart* **Audio Training** (secret formulas for speed copywriting)...

- **The one-page copywriting guide** (the basics of copywriting "at-a-glance")...

- **The one-page headline guide** (a quick "cheat sheet" for writing killer headlines)...

Claim your free training now...
RayEdwards.com/moneywords

Introduction

Confessions of a Hope Fiend

I admit it. I sell hope. You might call me a dealer. I'm okay with that. Call it optimism if you will. I like to think of my business in general, and copywriting in particular, as encouraging other people to live out their best potential.

There are those who are critical of this mindset, those who are quick to point out everything that is wrong with the world. The economy. Human trafficking. The shifting of global power. Pollution. The health crisis.

They have a point. Where we differ is how we approach all these problems.

I believe that hope gives birth to answers.

It gives us access to the resources we need (both internal and external) to start solving those problems.

I believe in acknowledging reality; I just don't believe in stopping there. Once we've identified the problem, it's time to start focusing on the solution.

A great writer once pointed out three essentials for living on the earth: faith, hope, and love. And while he said that the greatest of these is love (and I agree), I believe that love is birthed when we mix faith and hope.

Optimists just spend less time dwelling on what's wrong with the world. They spend less time thinking about what might go wrong with their plans.

Sometimes they fall on their faces.

But everything we love about the world originated in the heart of an optimist.

You might think that is overstating the case. But I happen to believe we were all created by the ultimate optimist: God.

He knew just how wrong the human race would be capable of going. How wrong we would go. But he saw something in us that he loved.

And he created us anyway. Gave us the capacity for faith, and for love, and for hope. That, my friend, is optimism. I like it.

So I'll just keep on selling hope. And I hope you will too.

Ray Edwards
Los Angeles, California
December, 2012

∽ MoneyWords™∽

Windfall Profits Hidden in Your Business

There is money hidden in your business. Money that you could be using. Money that, unless you do something about it, will slip through your fingers and vanish without a trace. Where is this money — and how do you get it?

Most businesses have many hidden opportunities for discovering "windfall profits" — but I want to focus on just one of those opportunities in this article. That "opportunity pocket" is marketing and advertising.

In my experience, almost every business — whether it be retail, service, professional practice, or "business to business" in its nature — is unconsciously letting profits slip away.

Your biggest opportunity most likely lies hidden inside your underperforming sales copy (copy that isn't selling as many units/ contracts/ memberships as it potentially could be).

If you want to make more sales without spending a single dime in additional ad costs, this article might be the most important document you read this year...

Make Piles of Money with "Upside Leverage"

"Upside Leverage" is a concept I learned from marketing genius Jay

Abraham. We all know what leverage is: using other people's money to build your business, or other people's efforts (through delegation, for instance) to increase your own productivity.

"Leverage" involves using one asset (the lever) to increase the value or power of another. The only problem with using "leverage" is the potential downside: if you use financial leverage to borrow money for a business project, the project could possibly fail, and you would be forced to pay back the money. If you use the leverage of delegation in order to make yourself more productive, there's a chance the person you're relying on might let you down.

"Upside" leverage is leverage that involves little or no potential downside.   It's my belief that underperforming sales copy is the most potentially profitable of all forms of "upside leverage."

Please read that sentence again, because it's too easy to let the profound meaning it contains slip past you:

Underperforming sales copy is the most potentially profitable of all forms of "upside leverage."

Think of it this way: any ad or promotion costs the same whether it performs well or not, right? If you spend $100 on an ad, and you get $500 in business as a result, you made a 5-1 return on your investment. That's a good return. You did what you set out to do: you made a profit.

But what if you could take that same ad, and change it in some way that made it 10 times more effective?

What if now it returned $5,000?

You spent the same $100 for the ad, but you got back $5,000.

Instead of a 5-1 return, now you're getting 50-1! That, my marketing friend, is "upside leverage"!

Change Your Copy, Change Your Income

There is so much bad copy on the web, it's almost laughably easy to be better than most of your competitors.

Why is that?

I believe there are a number of reasons, but here are a few of the common ones:

1. **Some people just don't realize their copy is bad.** They wrote it themselves, or their brother or their niece wrote it. They think it's wonderful — but in reality it stinks like a dead skunk.

2. **Others don't realize how important their sales copy is.** This is a naive belief, and it astounds me that so many people hold it — but they do. Some people seem to think that as long as the copy has "just the facts," that'll be good enough. It never is.

3. **Some people are just cheap.** They spend hundreds of thousands of dollars to start a business, buy furniture, hire staff, provide benefits, etc., but when it comes to the one piece of communication that might actually cause someone to buy from them, they don't want to pay for it. They "delegate" this crucial task. Big mistake.

Are you making any of these mistakes? If you are, this is your wake-up call.

Take advantage of the potential "upside leverage" that exists in every ad or promotion. Make sure your ads are performing — that they are making you sales every day. And that they are making you more sales this week than they did last week, etc.

You do this through constant improvement and testing/tracking.

You also do it by either hiring a copywriter or investing in educational materials that will teach you how to write your own copy. Either one can work — it's up to you. If you love to write, and you think you have a knack for it, then by all means get a good home-study course on copywriting and do it yourself.

Don't put it off — do it right now. Otherwise, you're throwing money away that rightfully belongs to you.

How to Decide What to Sell Online

"Ray, what do I sell online? How do I decide?" This is a question I am asked often, and my answer to this question is in two parts.

First is an answer appropriate if you're already selling something online, and the second part is the answer for those of you who haven't yet decided what product or service you're going to sell.

Let's start with the first situation. You're already selling something — a product or service — online. If you want to re-energize your business, you simply find a new product line or service to offer your existing customers.

Survey those existing customers and ask them what their needs are. You can use a service like SurveyMonkey.com, which is a very simple way to survey your customers that also offers some sophisticated data analysis tools.

So when you're surveying your present customers, what exactly do you ask them? You might want to start with something simple. First, determine what your category is. If you have an existing business that sells dog-training materials, for instance, you might do a simple survey where you ask your customers, what's your biggest problem when it comes to dog training?

Now, what if you're not already selling something online and you're trying to determine what your product or service is going to be? The answer is remarkably similar. In this case you also want to do a survey, but this time you're going to survey yourself, your colleagues, friends, and associates.

What are you looking for? You're looking for things that you're both good at and passionate about... that others will pay for. If you can find that combination, you'll have a much clearer idea of what you should be marketing. Here's the exercise:

Sit down with two clean sheets of paper and ask yourself this question. "What am I good at?" Make a list. Your list might include things like:

- Teaching
- Writing
- Graphic design
- Ideas
- Connecting with people
- Etc.

Don't make any judgments about which of these things might be marketable. That will come later. For now, just write down a long list of things you're good at — even the little things, like organizing your daily tasks, keeping your home or office in order, or even playing video games!

On the second sheet of paper, answer this question: "What am I passionate about?"

This list may surprise you. You may have written down that you're good at keeping your checkbook up to date — but now you may write down that you hate accounting! Don't worry about it. Just keep writing.

Make this second list as long as you can, and then compare the two and see if there are any items that show up on both lists. You want to pay attention, because these may be potential areas where you want to focus your efforts.

Now I want you to ask your colleagues, friends, and associates a similar question. Ask them to tell you what you're good at. Don't prejudice their answers; just get their initial first impressions of what they think you're good at.

Then compile those answers and again go back to your other lists. The things that show up on all the lists will give you some big clues of what you want to focus on and what you want to sell online as a product or service.

I believe that focusing on an area that you're both good at and passionate about is the best answer.

There are those who recommend focusing only on where there's a market need. Those who hold this opinion would say that your personal preference doesn't matter.

While it's true that you must be careful not to make the entire decision based only on your feelings, I don't think it's wise to disregard them either. Do you want to be stuck with a successful business that you hate?

My opinion is that if you want to stick with your business and remain excited about it, and if you want the joy as well as the money, focus on something you're good at and that you're passionate about.

4

What You Really Get Paid For

This chapter is only for those who already have a website that's making money online.

I'm about to show you how you can double or triple your conversions without lifting a finger.

Seriously. So, if you have a money-making site online right now, keep reading.

The rest of you may be excused (sorry, just figured I might as well be up front about who this is for).

Here's the deal...

Have you ever heard that story about the ocean-going ship engine that failed?

In the version I heard, it was the Queen Elizabeth luxury liner.

The vessel's owners brought in all their on-staff engineers to fix it, but none of them could get the engine running.

Finally, they brought in an expert who had been fixing ships all his life. The old expert hauled in his bag of tools and looked around a bit.

He crawled all over that engine room, looking, touching, and thinking.

Finally, he went to his bag, pulled out a small hammer, and tapped a few times on a valve. The engine roared to life.

A week later, the owners of the ship received a bill for ten thousand dollars.

They were outraged. After all, the man had only tapped on a valve with a hammer!

They immediately demanded he send them an itemized bill explaining his charges. He sent them a bill that read:

"Tapping with a hammer..................... $2
Knowing where to tap.................. $9,998"

Knowing where to tap is important to your sales copy, too.

The simplest changes can make the most profound difference in your results.

There is an art to writing copy, but there is also a science to getting the maximum result. And that science is called "testing."

Here's the "magic formula": get a sales letter that makes SOME money. That gets SOME conversions and sales.

Then TEST the heck out of new headlines, deck copy, subheads, offers, guarantees, pictures, etc. In other words, use the ART of copywriting plus the SCIENCE of testing to find out...WHERE TO TAP.

As marketers and copywriters, knowing "where to tap" is what we get paid for.

5 Deadly Copywriting Mistakes That Kill Your Sales

Chances are you are making many — if not all — of these 5 copywriting mistakes. I call them "deadly" because they're killing your sales and your profits.

Let me make you a bold promise: examine your own sales copy and eliminate these copywriting mistakes, and you will see an instant improvement in your sales.

Let's get started...

Deadly Mistake #1:
Being Focused on You, Instead of Your Market

This is the easiest mistake to make and the most common. Most ad copy is focused on the advertiser, not on the consumer. Big mistake.

When you read copy that says things like, "We're the best in the industry... we've been in business since 1979... we have the most well-trained associates... our facility has won many industry awards, etc."... what is your reaction?

Most likely, your reaction is, "So what? What does that mean to me and my life?"

If you're using copy that says "we," "us," and "our" a lot, find a way to change that copy so that it says "you," and "yours." Speak about the things that matter to your customer.

Here's a hint: those things are probably not what you think they are. Why not ask your customers? They know the answer, and they'll be glad to share it with you if you're wise enough to listen.

Deadly Mistake #2:
Using a Weak, Wimpy, or Just Plain Bad Headline

In the beginning, you only have one chance to grab the reader's attention. That chance is the headline. Make sure your headline is strong, aggressive (without being pushy), and compelling.

Think of your headline as the sales pitch to get the prospect to read the whole ad. It has to be compelling enough that the reader thinks, "Hey, if this is true, I need to know about it…"

You get one shot. You can't afford to blow it.

A poor headline for an automotive shop: "Our Experienced Staff Can Tend to Your Every Automotive Need, And Are ASE Certified with the Guaranteed Lowest Prices."

A much better headline for the same client: "Are Hidden Mechanical Problems with Your Car Threatening the Health and Safety of Your Family? Our 9-Point Safety Inspection Could Save Their Lives — and Give You Peace of Mind."

Deadly Mistake #3:
Not Using Enough Bullets

Bullets break up your copy into short, readable bursts. Especially on the web, people tend to scan copy before they read it; breaking your benefits into bullets increases the chances your copy will "catch the eye" and thus get read. To recap the benefits of bullets:

- They break up copy (just like this) into short pieces.
- They make the copy easier to scan.
- They make it easier to pick out key words and phrases.

- They get more of your copy read.
- They make you more sales.
- The more bullets the better (usually).

Deadly Mistake #4:
Using Big Words and Jargon

Copy should read like conversation; it should flow naturally and be easy to process.

Using big words and jargon might sound impressive, but it won't get you sales. Which would you prefer?

Use strong, punchy words. Write simply and clearly.

Read Strunk & White's Elements of Style — and follow its advice. Avoid jargon.

Deadly Mistake #5:
Using Weak, Wimpy, or Just Plain Bad Subheads

You should use subheads every 3-4 paragraphs in your copy.

Make subheads strong and compelling; think of them as headlines for each section of your copy.

If read in sequence, your subheads should sound like an abbreviated version of your sales pitch (which is what they are).

Subheads done correctly are a way to "stop the eye," catch the reader's interest, and get him to slow down enough to read that section.

What to Do Now

Here's your "takeaway" from this chapter: grab your own current sales copy, this list of copy mistakes, your favorite beverage, and go through your copy line-by-line.

Ferret out these mistakes and eliminate them from your copy. Do it now, and don't put it off.

6

Another 5 Mistakes That Kill Your Sales

This is "Part 2" of the previous chapter, so we'll pick it up with #6...

Deadly Mistake #6:
Sentences and Paragraphs That Are Too Long

Keep your sentences and your paragraphs short.

A paragraph in a sales letter should be no more than 3-4 sentences long — and they should be short sentences.

People will read more of your copy if the sentences and paragraphs are short. This is especially important on the first page (or the first screen, if it's online) of your sales letter, when you are trying to draw them into your story.

Don't scare people off with big blocks of text.

Deadly Mistake #7:
Not Enough Testimonials

One of your first tasks as a copywriter is to break down that skepticism and get them to believe you — even just a little bit.

Once that initial barrier of skepticism comes down, you have a chance of making a sale. How do you break through that skepticism?

Testimonials

You need lots of testimonials in your copy. How many? As many as you can get.

Here's a good rule of thumb: however many you have now, get 25 % more.

Deadly Mistake #8:
Offers That Stink

If your offer stinks, the best copy in the world won't help you.

By your offer, I mean the bundle, widget, or information as presented for sale. This includes your price and how you demonstrate the value of your offer versus what you're charging for it.

It's best if you're in the position of "selling dollars for dimes." Then it's easy to show the value of your offer.

For instance, if you sell a device that causes a 20% increase in a car's fuel efficiency, you might frame the offer like this: "The Fuel-Saver is $99 — but you'll save ten times that amount per year in fuel costs. So you get back more than TEN TIMES YOUR INVEST-MENT in just one year!"

Is your offer good? If not, figure out how to make it good!

Deadly Mistake #9:
Forgetting to Ask for the Sale

It's one of the most common mistakes in all forms of selling — not asking for the sale. Hard to believe? Maybe. But it's true anyway; people just don't want to ask for the order.

There comes a point where you've presented all the benefits of your offer; you've demonstrated its value, you've supplied lots of credible testimonials, you've shown your iron-clad guarantee… and you just need to ask for the sale.

On the Internet, this can be as easy as putting in a link that says "Order Now."

Online Marketer Armand Morin often has 5-7 order links on each of his sales pages; he says that the more "order links" he adds, the more sales he makes.

Deadly Mistake #10:
Pricing Before Benefits and Offer

Sometimes business owners want to use price point as a selling feature, and so you see lots of web pages that right near the top will say something like "Now Only $24.95!"

That's a deadly mistake.

First, you are signaling readers that this page is an ad, not a page of information. That will cause you to lose readers before you've had a chance to tell them your story.

Second, you haven't had a chance to elaborate on the benefits of your product or service or to show the value of your offer.

Long before the price ever shows up on your page, you need to make prospects feel that they must have the benefits that your product offers.

They must desire those benefits in a strong and intense way.

Don't reveal your price before you spell out the benefits of your product and the value of your offer. If you do this well, and you do it in the correct order, price will never be an objection; your offer will always seem like a bargain.

Just as with the previous chapter, you need to go through your copy line-by-line. Ferret out these mistakes and eliminate them.

7

3 Ways to Break Through Skepticism

You probably don't need me to tell you this, but prospects are more skeptical online than ever before.

The Holy Grail of online marketing is getting the prospect's email address (so you can start building a permission-based marketing relationship with them).

In the not-too-distant past, you could generate leads online simply by offering a free newsletter or special report. This doesn't work so well anymore.

Why? The reason is simple: there's too much 'junk' being offered, and prospects are wise to this. People just won't give up their email address for a junky 'special report' like they used to.

So what's a marketer to do? Here are three ways to break through skepticism and get your prospects to give you their email addresses:

1. Offer Superior Premiums

Offering a superior premium will help you "cut through the clutter," but to be effective, your premium must be clearly superior.

Commonplace and boring:

"Special Reports" and "Free Tele-Seminars"

Better:

Software that performs a specific task, a free telephone consultation (make it clear this is not a sales pitch), or a free membership website

2. Use Video Testimonials

There's a reason infomercial producers make their 30-minute ads over 70% testimonials: testimonials overcome skepticism.

These days, it's cheap and easy to make video testimonials for your website. Get your best customers singing your praises on video, and put these snippets on your website–lots of them.

3. Use the "Reciprocity Sequence Method"

You've no doubt heard of the 'Reciprocity' principal: if I give you a gift, you feel compelled to reciprocate.

The trouble is, your prospects often have heard of it too, rendering it somewhat less effective.

I use a technique I call the "Reciprocity Sequence Method"... which is simply giving your prospects a series of gifts so that the "Reciprocity Impulse" becomes almost overwhelming. It sounds elementary, but few people do it. It's very powerful.

Think about how you can 'stack' a sequence of 3-5 gifts in a short period of time, and THEN make an offer to your prospect.

Key points to remember:

1. Keep the sequence confined to a short time period.
2. Make the gifts relevant to (and an enhancement of) your core offer.

3.   Make the offer immediately after giving the final gift.

While it's true that skepticism is at a higher level than ever, it's also true that breaking through is easy when you know how.

8

The Master Key to Success

How many times have you heard self-help or business gurus talk about how they 'uncovered' the 'real secrets' of success? Hundreds? Thousands?

Well, let me save you some money and time. Forget the gurus for a moment. Here is the real, true, 'Master Secret of Success':

Just Get Started!

Don't laugh. The problem most business people, entrepreneurs, and companies have is that they spend far too much time coming up with new buzzwords and management systems — and almost zero time just getting down to the work that needs to be done.

For the individual or entrepreneur, I offer this tactic that will help you 'get started' on something that will generate new revenue...

Think carefully about your answer to this question:

If you could only do one thing to generate revenue immediately, what would that one thing be?

I really want you to think about this. If it was a "must have"–for instance, if it meant being able to pay the mortgage on your house this month–what one thing would you do right now?

Some possible examples:

- Write a letter and mail it.
- Make a phone call.
- Send an email.
- Drive to see a prospect in person.
- Complete and deliver a proposal.

Okay, do you have your "one thing"? Great! *Write it down*. Then... JUST GET STARTED! When it's done, do the whole exercise over again.

I know that right about now you're thinking, "Ray, this is the most elementary, simple, stupid thing I've heard all week."

That's okay. Try it anyway–and after you have tried it, I'd love to hear from you with your success story.

And remember, you heard the Master Key to Success right here. In case you forgot already, it's this:

Just Get Started!

9

Just Get Started, Part 2

I recently attended Dr Mike Woo-Ming and Howard Schwartz's "AdSense Immersion" seminar in New York.

People paid big bucks to be there, it was a small group...and you'd be surprised at how many "gurus" were in the room. Mike Filsaime was there. So were Carl Galletti, Rick Butts, and Len Thurmond... and that was just the tip of the iceberg. Why am I telling you this? Two reasons:

1. **If you want to be successful, you must never stop learning.** No matter how successful you already are, attending seminars and conferences "works." You learn things that can help you make money.

2. **It's up to you to do something with what you learn.** Information alone does not create profit–profit is only created when you take action.

A common theme we discussed at the conference was how all of us have tons of information and software — but we're not using it. Yet when the "new thing" comes out, we all rush to buy it.

Problem is, we still haven't used the last "new thing" we bought!

Think about it...how many conferences have you attended in the last year? How many pages of notes did you take? How many information products did you buy?

How's all that working out for you? Did you take action on all the stuff you made notes about? Did you implement the strategies and tactics you learned in the information products you bought? Did you even open the information products you bought? It's okay– we're all "guilty," to some extent.

"Bonus tip" and "mini-action plan"

TIP: Take stock of all your notes,
information products, and memberships.

ACTION PLAN

1. Set aside a small amount of time each day for the next couple of weeks.

2. Each day, pick one set of notes... one information product... or one membership site...and go to work.

3. Implement just one step, strategy, or tactic. Just one.

I predict that if you do this, you'll experience quick, profitable growth in your business.

Just get started.

10

3 Simple Ways to Get Started With Testing

If you've been around the direct marketing business very long, you've heard the advice that you must test your marketing.

I am frequently asked, "Ray, how do I get started with testing?" Here are 3 simple ways you can start testing today–without complex math, expensive software, or arcane technology.

1. **Test your current headline against a new one.** Don't worry about getting software or other tools just yet. Simply run one headline for a while — then run the other headline for an equal amount of time. If you can run equal amounts of traffic past both headlines, you will have at least a general idea which one works best.

2. **Test your current price against a higher one.** That's right — I said higher. If the higher price loses the test, THEN test a lower price. It may surprise you that higher prices often bring more orders! So, this week, track your numbers at your current price — and next week test a higher one.

3. **If you use graphics on your page, test the page without a header graphic.** Often, the page without the header will

produce more results. The theory is that the graphic distracts from the copy. It is possibly causing your prospect to bypass reading the headline. Don't accept the theory–test it yourself.

It is true that to do mathematically reliable tests, you will need some kind of software to track the results.

If you're not doing any testing at all, start with these 3 simple tests. You may end up increasing your profits!

11

Write 3 Killer Headlines in 3 Minutes

If you've studied copywriting very long, you know that the most important copy on the page is the headline. That's because the headline is the ad that gets prospects to read the rest of the ad.

How can you write effective headlines if you're not a professional copywriter? Simple–use "template" headlines as starting point.

I've provided 3 template headlines below. Fill in the blanks as appropriate for your product offer. You may need to do some re-wording to make the headline work for your product–but you'll be off to a good start.

TEMPLATE HEADLINE:

> **Give Me (amount of time) and**
> **I'll Give You (benefit of product)**

Example: Give Me 3 Minutes, and I'll Show You How to Write 3 Killer Headlines

TEMPLATE HEADLINE:

> **If You Can (something simple prospect can do),**
> **Then You Can (benefit product can produce)**

Example: If You Can Send and Receive Email, Then You Can Make Money with My Email Marketing Course.

TEMPLATE HEADLINE:

Who Else Wants to (benefit product produces)?

Example: Who Else Wants to Double Your Sales — and Triple Your Time Off?

12

Jump Starters for Writing Killer Copy

Do you find yourself staring at a blank screen, wondering how to get started writing your copy?

I've found that I get much better results if I use some "jump starters" — they keep me focused and get me started on the right track with a copy project.

Here are 3 "tricks" I use — maybe they'll work for you, too:

Write the benefit bullets.

Don't worry about writing body copy just yet. Just start banging out all the benefits of owning the product. This will be a more extensive list than the one in the order box (which is our next "jump starter").

Write the order box copy.

This is the part of the copy where you clearly spell out the price of your offer and the bullet points showing the main benefits of owning the product. Select the MAIN benefits (the ones with the most "persuasion power") for the order box.

Write 10 possible headlines for your copy.

Don't worry if they're not "good enough." You can even use some of the bullets you've written as starting points. Use a headline "swipe file" to spark ideas. Just get 10 headlines written.

Once you've finished these 3 "jump starters," you will have written quite a bit of copy. It will be focused on the benefits of owning the product. You'll be off to a good start on your copy project.

13

Is Your Copy Filled With Hype?

Do you worry that your copy might be too "hypey"?

Dictionary.com defines "hype" as "an ingenious or questionable claim, method, etc., used in advertising, promotion, or publicity to intensify the effect."

One of the additional definitions is "a swindle, deception, or trick."

I rather think the second one is what we have in mind when we say a copy is full of hype.

There is a place for the kind of hype that is "an ingenious...claim, method, etc., used in advertising, promotion, or publicity to intensify the effect."

There is not a place in a respectable copywriter's toolbox for the kind of hype that is "questionable" or that uses "deception or tricks."

The most reliable test for whether your copy is filled with the "bad" kind of hype is simple: is the claim being made in the copy true? If so, and if you can prove that it's true, then it's not the "bad" kind of hype.

What's more, if your copy is presented to the true prospects for your product or service, it won't be perceived as hype.

14

1 Simple Trick to Strengthen Your Copy

Want to make your copy stronger with one simple trick?

Eliminate all the adverbs.

What's an adverb? It's a word–often ending in the letters "ly"–that modifies a verb (or even adjectives or adverbial phrases). Examples of adverbs: quickly, instantly, amazingly, powerfully.

If you find the above passage puzzling, don't worry about it; just go through your copy and try to eliminate as many of those "ly" words as you can.

Here's an example:

"Quickly and easily motivate clients to buy stuff." becomes

"Motivate clients to buy stuff."

Now you may be tempted to ask: "But Ray, I want them to know it happens quickly and easily!" No problem. Just be specific.

Example:

"Motivate clients to buy stuff starting the minute you install the software, without any extra effort on your part."

You may need to do a bit of rewriting to make the copy flow without the adverbs, but your language will be stronger and more persuasive for the effort.

15

3 Mistakes That Kill Copy

There are 3 mistakes made by most advertising copy I see that depress sales and response. Correct these mistakes and increase your sales.

1: Focusing On You, Not Your Customer

In the context of an ad, your prospects don't care about you. They care about themselves, and whether your product can help solve their problem(s).

Look for and eliminate phrases like: 'our friendly staff,' '20 years in business,' 'for all your [INSERT PRODUCT HERE] needs.'

Those are about you. Use phrases that speak to the solution to your prospect's most pressing problems.

2: Using Cliché Language

Clichés are like wallpaper, nobody notices them unless they're so bad they can't be ignored.

Some clichés to look for: 'giant blow out,' 'explode your sales,' 'save like never before,' 'savings throughout the store'... There are too many advertising clichés to list here.

You probably recognize them when you hear them.

Get them out of your copy.

3: Speaking Inappropriately

No, this doesn't mean correcting your grammar–unless your intended audience is English teachers.

Speaking inappropriately means using language patterns that cause your audience to disagree with you on some minor subject. Once that happens, it will be much more difficult to get their agreement on a more important topic (such as buying your product).

For example, if you are selling to English teachers and you use poor grammar in your copy, it will be much harder to make the sale (even if the sale has nothing to do with grammar).

Why? Because you have lost credibility with your audience–you are not 'speaking their language.'

16

The Writer's Life

There is a myth in the marketing world that anyone can write copy.

Myth #1: Anyone can write good copy.

When this myth is spoken, it's usually followed by the advice that 'all one needs is a good swipe file' (successful ads of the past that one can "borrow" from).

This has always struck me as false — or at least only partially true.

I believe that when it comes right down to it, you must have some writing talent. If you don't, your copy will not be brilliant. It may not even be good. In most cases, it will just be bad.

I see plenty of evidence that the last is the most common result.

Myth #2: If one studies enough of the right manuals, or attends enough of the right seminars, one can learn to write well.

Frankly, if you don't have some native talent — a "knack," if you will — I don't think all the classes, courses, or seminars in the world can help you much.

Stephen King would agree with me, I suspect. In a recent article he penned for the Washington Post, King wrote, "The only things that can teach writing are reading, writing and the semi-domestication of one's muse."

My opinion is that not everyone can learn to be a great (or even a good) writer. Everyone is born with a certain aptitude (or lack of it), and they're pretty much stuck with that aptitude. They can take classes or be taught to make the most of it, but they are always limited to a certain range in the development of their craft.

17

Breaking Through Writer's Block

I have to be honest: I don't believe in "writer's block." You shouldn't either. I think it's another myth. Worse, I think it's an excuse for just not doing your job.

I'm not saying that it isn't sometimes difficult to sit down and start writing. It often is difficult, for one reason or another. The same could be said of a plumber, a carpenter, or even a doctor.

Have you ever heard of a surgeon saying, "I just can't do this surgery today. I've got surgeon's block"? Of course not!

There are undoubtedly days where even surgeons don't feel like doing their job. Maybe they're distracted, they're tired, or they have other things on their minds. There is no such thing as "surgeon's block"... or "writer's block."

What should you do on days when you just don't feel like writing anything? I've found the quickest cure is to decide: there's no such thing as writer's block... and just start writing. Write anything.

Start with the easy stuff.

- Write the contact information that's going to go on your sales letter or website.
- Write the copyright information.

- Write filler text such as "Insert Brilliant Headline Here."
- Write the details of what you're offering. I'm talking about the simple stuff you don't have to think in order to write.
- What's the price?
- What's the address of your company?
- Where do customers send the checks?

Just start writing.

Once you've loosened up a bit, start writing some bullet points. Write as many bullets as you possibly can, remembering to keep each of them focused on benefits of the product (not just features of the product).

You can just write pages of bullets and eventually you'll get into the flow of writing.

Most of the time, you'll discover you can use a lot of the bullets you've written as thought starters for headlines, for subheads, for section heads, etc. Heck, maybe you'll even use them as bullets.

And guess what? Now you've "broken through your writer's block."

18

Email Marketing: Dead or Alive?

Many people say email marketing is dead. It's easy to agree with this idea. Spam and the spam filters it has given rise to make it harder than ever to get your email delivered.

It's even hard to receive email we want. How many times have you been frustrated because a friend, co-worker, or relative was supposed to send you an email that never arrived... only to discover that email in your "junk mail" or "spam" folder? Here's the good news:

The death of email marketing has been greatly exaggerated.

Even though deliverability rates are lower than ever, email marketing still works and is still responsible for many millions of dollars worth of sales. It can work for you as well.

3 Keys to Successful Email Marketing

1: Keep a clean double opt-in email list.

What this means is that if someone signs up to receive email from you, you need to get them to confirm that they actually want to receive the email.

Most email marketing providers, (like aweber and 1Shopping-Cart) automatically require people to double opt in to any email list.

In some cases the "double opt-in" feature is optional... but I think it's the best way to manage your email list.

Single opt-in (no confirmation required) may yield bigger subscriber numbers (it does), but that list will be less responsive to your offers.

2: Educate your customers on how to white-list or authorize your emails to get through to their inbox.

Usually this is just a case of having them put your email address into their address book; if they use a service like Spam Arrest they'll have to go to the actual website and authorize your email address. Teach them how to do that, either using text and illustrations or with screen capture video.

3: Boost response rates to your messages.

How do you do this? Make sure you send relevant and expected content to your email list.

Emailing your list frequently will get your emails through more readily and get you a lot fewer spam complaints. Why?

Because if you send frequently, people are going to do one of two things: read your email or unsubscribe.

If you email them less frequently, you run the risk that they will forget who you are or even forget that they subscribed to your list... and that will generate spam complaints.

Use these keys to successful email marketing and watch your list numbers and response rates grow.

Long live email marketing!

19

Hemingway's 4 Rules of Writing

Here's what I have in common with Papa Hemingway: I love words, and I'm a writer.

When it comes to writing ads (and when I say ads, I mean everything from web pages to emails to postcards!), it's hard to find better advice than Ernest Hemingway's 4 Rules of Writing.

Hemingway's 4 Rules of Writing

1. Use short sentences.
2. Use short first paragraphs.
3. Use vigorous English.
4. Be positive, not negative.

Those rules are posted on the wall behind my computer monitor. You may want to post them near yours.

20

Do Squeeze Pages Still Work for List-Building?

Should you use a "squeeze page" on your website, or have these pages lost their effectiveness?

A "squeeze page" is one that forces your site visitors to give you their name and email address in exchange for some kind of bribe... an audio training, a special report, or piece of software.

Making a free offer to your site visitors in exchange for their names and email addresses is a great way to grow your email list, but it has to be done carefully so that you don't also drive away potential customers.

Here are some things to think about...

You know it's important to grow your email list. The bigger the list, the more people will see your offers, and the more money you will make. The challenge in today's internet marketing world is that it's harder than ever to convince people to opt in.

A squeeze page is probably the best list-building tool available, but you must be careful. Using a squeeze page the wrong way can hurt your business more than it helps.

It's best to use a squeeze page on a site that is built to sell one product.

For example, if you have a site that features a sales letter selling a particular product or service, placing a squeeze page in front of the information about that product or service is a good idea.

This keeps readers from being distracted. It sifts and sorts potential buyers by level of seriousness and it gives you a list of interested parties that you can go back and market to repeatedly.

One of the biggest mistakes I see being made online is putting a squeeze page in front of the wrong kinds of sites.

Don't put a squeeze page in front of your portal site, your branding site, or your blog.

Putting a squeeze page in front of those kinds of sites does not make sense. Those sites have a very different purpose than sites that are intended to sell one targeted product or promotion.

Remember that your squeeze page is a gate. It keeps people out of your website, and it can potentially scare off your customers.

If you have a strong enough offer, a video, an audio, or special report, you may be able to get people to opt in and build a very targeted list using a squeeze page.

The growing problems of spam, viruses and spyware have made people more reluctant than ever to give up their names and email addresses.

Squeeze pages can definitely build your list fast. These pages are a powerful tool that I recommend to all of my clients; just be sure to use them in the appropriate situation.

21

5 Easy Ways to Scan Your Market's Brain

You need content for your blog or newsletter or ezine.

It needs to be relevant — in other words, you need to write about stuff your market cares about.

Most bloggers (newsletter/ezine publishers, speakers, authors, etc.) don't have a clue what their market cares about. Oh, they think they know what the market wants. That's the problem.

Don't be too upset if this has happened to you, because I'm about to give you 5 easy ways to always know exactly what's on the mind of your market.

It's almost as if they were wearing signs around their necks proclaiming, "Here's what has my attention right now." This is going to seem brain-dead simple.

Find out what they're already talking about, or what they're already paying attention to, and give them more of that.

But with your own unique spin and of course, in a way that adds value to their lives (and at the same time leads them to your door).

Just look at these 5 websites that are like magical marketing X-ray machines to see what's inside the mind of your market.

1. http://del.icio.us
2. http://digg.com
3. http://answers.yahoo.com
4. http://stumbleupon.com
5. http://google.com/news

Of course, it's up to you (or your copywriter) to figure out how and why today's hot topics matter to your market. And how they relate to your message about who you are and what you bring to the world.

22

How to Go from "Surviving" to "Thriving"

It astounds me, but at every seminar I attend, someone asks me this question: "Does anybody really make a living selling information online?"

I also hear this one: "You can't make any money as a copywriter or marketer now that the economy has gone down the toilet." What a load of garbage! Aaarrrgh! Here's why...

It's easier than ever to make money online.

If you're a copywriter, it is especially easy to make money online. Why would I say that? Simple. If you know how to write great copy, you have three ways to make money online:

1. You can get paid to write copy for others.

2. You can make money writing copy for your own products that you sell online (that may have nothing to do with copywriting or marketing).

3. You can make money as an affiliate for other people's products (because you have copy skills, your promos will be far more effective than those of mere mortal marketers).

Not one way to make income, but three ways

You might think I'm exaggerating. Heck, you might even think I'm lying. It doesn't matter, because I'm proving every day that what I'm saying is true.

I look around me and I see lots of evidence that the "economy" has not "stopped" the wheels of commerce.

For instance, during the height of the economic crash, I traveled the country in my new motor home. In 2 months I had visited both Disney parks in the USA (Disney World in Florida, and Disney Land in California) plus I'd been to Las Vegas, Phoenix, and a few other sunny places.

At one point, I looked out my window and I saw lots of motor homes (which cost $80,000–$700,000 or more). Nobody told all these people the economy was "in trouble."

And while I was in Vegas, I visited the Coach store, the Apple Store, and many others. Crammed with people spending money.

Now, some people are spending money, right? OBVIOUSLY.

And just as in the retail business, the RV business, the exotic car business…and the marketing business, people are still buying.

(Look, I'm not minimizing anyone's pain here; I understand that there are many people experiencing real problems. Far from criticizing them or minimizing the seriousness of their situation, I'm simply pointing to one possible way out of those problems.)

And the good news, if you're a copywriter, is that you have three ways to make money.

Trust me, other marketers will pay you LOADS to write killer copy for them because they hate writing their own, in most cases.

It gets even better

When you can write your own copy, you can roll out as many of your own products as you like. One little online money machine after another. See how that works?

And because you write YOUR OWN COPY, you bypass the single

biggest expense in marketing: copy.

So my message is really quite simple: whatever you have to do... GET GOOD AT WRITING COPY. It's the one skill that pays you back for the rest of your life. I know it has for me. So do what it takes. Get good at copy.

If you need fast cash, you can write for other people.

Then, if you want to build long-term income, write copy for your own products and/or promote affiliate products.

It's the winning skill in today's "economy."

23

Copywriting Monkey

The discussion turned to "back end promotions." This means "what you sell people after they bought your entry-level product."

The topic was the copy used to sell back-end promotions. One of the well-known, high-profile marketers on the call said something like, "Heck, you don't need a great copywriter to write that stuff. Those people are already your customers. A monkey could write that stuff."

(BUZZER.) That player is out of the game. If you think any piece of your copy can be written by "a monkey," you're in trouble. If that's what you think, you're saying your customers are monkeys, too. See how that works?

And if you still think there's nothing wrong with all that, try this exercise:

Imagine your mother or your grandmother is the customer in question. Now imagine telling Mom or Grandma you hired a monkey to handle this part of their transaction, because that's all the respect you needed to give them.

How's that working for you?

24

Freelancers: Do Clients Suck?

This one is for those of us who are freelancers, service providers, or who have ongoing relationships where we work with clients.

Gary Halbert–one of the greatest copywriters to ever work in the field–used to wear a hat that had two words embroidered on it: "Clients Suck."

Do they? A lot of people say they do. For a long time I bought into that idea. I had good reasons: most of my clients seemed to be too demanding, too unwilling to follow my advice, and too determined to carry out some weird idea even though it was clearly not in their best interest.

Some of my clients were even abusive, taking advantage of me in ways I don't want to go into here (it wouldn't help anybody to do so).

Then one day I realized I was making a contribution to each of those relationships that helped create that situation. My contribution was three-fold, and it directly contributed to making those relationships miserable for me (though they were, in fact, great for my clients).

One lesson for you: if the relationship is only great on one side... it's not great. It's dysfunctional, and somebody is getting hurt.

Here are the three things I was doing that made it seem as though "clients suck":

1. Not carefully selecting clients from the beginning, screening out those with whom I was not a good match.

2. Not setting boundaries for the relationship so that both parties know what those boundaries are and the reasons they are in place.

3. Not realizing that I was free to "fire" clients who were "problem children."

Once I finally figured those three things out, I changed the way I selected clients, how I set boundaries with them, and how I communicated with them when those boundaries were crossed.

I was completely freed from the notion that "clients suck," because mine don't suck now.

That's the lesson: you too can quickly reach a place where you love and appreciate your clients, where they don't trample on your schedule or your values, and where you can easily resolve any conflicts that might arise.

All You Have to Do Is: Develop criteria that describe your ideal client and use those criteria to screen out any clients who don't meet them.

1. Carefully and respectfully set the boundaries in your relationship from the beginning–and stick to them.

2. Communicate immediately with the client when those boundaries are crossed.

3. When you suspect that you need to "fire" a client, do it sooner rather than later. Trust me; you'll know when it is time.

If you will do those things, then when someone says to you that "clients suck," you'll be able to give them the same response I do: "Mine don't."

25

The Magic Formula for Writing
Copy That Sells

Many people want to know the "magic formula" is for writing web-sites and ad copy that sells. If you're one of those folks who would like to know that formula, I have some disappointing news: there isn't one.

"But Ray," I hear you say, "haven't you yourself taught several different copywriting 'formulas'?" Yes, but they are not "magic," and they don't work universally.

What a formula can do is give you a basic structure on which to hang your "argument" (your logic for why someone should buy your stuff).

What the formula cannot do is somehow magically compel people to buy something they don't really want or need. What a formula can't do is teach you the fears and aspirations of your readers, so that your persuasion power comes from the point of intersection between your audience's needs/desires and your product's features/benefits.

Only you, as an empathetic writer, can do that.

26

How to Read Minds

Most copywriters and marketers would agree that if you could read your prospect's mind, you could be a lot more successful writing copy for, and selling stuff to those prospects because you'd know their world.

You'd understand their pain. You'd know their deepest fears, and you'd understand their highest aspirations.

So how do you do that? Here are 7 practical tips. They sound simple, but when you actually use them, their impact can be profound.

1: Learn everything you can about your prospect.

If you're in direct marketing, it's easy: just look at their data cards. When you have demographics, you can infer a lot about the "average" person who represents the group. If you don't have that kind of data... guess.

It's a lot more accurate than what most marketers do (which is: they don't bother with any of this stuff).

2: Imagine yourself living your prospect's typical day.

Go through it step by step–from rising out of bed in the morning to getting back into the sack at night. Use all five of your senses:

What do you see, hear, feel, taste, touch and smell? Make notes.

3: Think about their biggest fear.

What is the one thing that wakes them up at 3 in the morning in a cold sweat?

4: Think about their highest aspiration.

What do they dream of? Not the little dreams (the ones we all tell our buddies), but the big dream in their "secret heart" (the dream that they don't dare tell anyone).

5: Go where they live.

Find a neighborhood that is like your prospect's and walk through it (driving doesn't work–looking at it through a window is just more TV... nice to look at but not REAL). Talk to people.

6: Read what they read.

Read their magazines, newspapers, blogs and Twitter.

7: Watch what they watch.

Watch the TV shows your prospects watch, especially the ones that don't interest you.

If you do this, you'll develop the apparent ability to read your prospect's mind. And you'll sell more.

Something funny about this is: you'll also most likely care more. And that's far more important than any selling technique. The world's a funny place, ain't it?

27

Number 1 Way to Make More Sales?

What's the number one way to make more sales? For better than 80% of companies (or freelancers, or salespeople, etc.) the answer is simple: so simple they're embarrassed to admit it.

The "secret" to getting more sales: ASK

For another 10-15 % "bump" in sales: when the prospect says "no," ask "why not?" Then answer their objection and ask for the sale again.

I know many will think this is oversimplified. Before you make that assumption, honestly ask yourself if you ask for the sale as often as you should.

28

Avoid the Obnoxious Bully Copywriter

If you're a copywriter, please take note: the "obnoxious bully copywriter persona" is overdone, possibly destructive and certainly no longer unique positioning.

You probably know what I'm talking about: the kind of copywriter who positions himself as a "badass" and a "rock star."

Usually this persona comes with a large dose of attitude. Often the persona is accompanied by disdain or even contempt for his customers — who are often portrayed by the "rock star copywriter" as mentally challenged at best and complete idiots at worst.

I hope you are not guilty of this, because it doesn't help anyone. It's also ugly and mean-spirited.

If you have been guilty of patterning yourself after a "badass copywriter," stop it. Just be yourself. Respect and honor your clients, and you will experience the prosperity you're after.

For the Clients of the Bully Copywriter

If you happen to be a client of one of these copywriters, or you're thinking of becoming a client of one, stop. Trust your gut. There are people who can write your copy and treat you with the respect and honor you deserve.

Take the time to find one of those people — and don't fall into a co-dependent relationship where you are the victim and the copy-writer is the bully.

29

Make Advertising a Profit Center
– Not an Expense

Most advertising is an expense — or worse — a mystery expense.

It works like this, most of the time: spend money on some ads, not knowing whether those ads will work, and hope for the best.

Ogilvy is famous for saying 50 % of his ads work — he just didn't know which 50%. It doesn't have to be this way.

You can make your advertising — and more importantly your marketing — a profit center instead of an expense. How do you do that?

Make it a No-Way-To-Lose proposition

1. Make sure each ad has a call to action you can measure (call this number, click this link).
2. Measure the response to each ad and each call to action.
3. Do more of the ones that work and less of the ones that don't.

This way you get something from every ad — even if the something is only knowledge of what not to do. You never lose; you always profit either by knowledge or dollars.

30

Mr. Spock's Guide to Sales

We buy because of emotion, and we justify the decision using logic.

Good sales people identify the emotion driving their prospect, and then line up the "reasons why" the purchase is a good idea. They use logic to close the sale, but logic is not making the sale.

Selling even worked with Captain Kirk on Star Trek

Kirk was a hot-head, you will remember. He wanted to spring into action. Spock, the non-emotional, scientific Vulcan, deftly supplied his Captain the logic needed to justify the decision.

Get this: Spock was the consummate sales person. A pro. Kirk was not.

Most sales people who turn us off are selling from the Captain Kirk School of Sales — all emotion, passion and pushiness.

The salespeople we love, the ones we happily buy from, are from the Mr. Spock School of Sales; they simply supply us with the logical reasons that support what we wanted to do already.

Be like Spock; supply the reasons why. It's the logical thing to do.

31

The $1,000 Barbecue Grill

You should charge more for whatever you sell. And you should be unapologetic about it.

That's true for probably 80 % of the students and clients I deal with, and for 90% or more of businesses I encounter along life's way.

"But Ray, my business is different." Aargh!

If I've heard it once, I've heard it a thousand times from clients and students in some variant form:

"I can't charge a high price for my product."

"I can't use direct marketing or info-marketing techniques, because my product is different."

"It's a commodity."

"It's physical; it's not an info-product."

"I have a lot of competition."

"Blah, blah, blah..."

Balderdash. I learned a long time ago from Dan Kennedy — your business is not different.

If you feel you can't charge a premium for whatever it is you sell, you have failed to differentiate your offer. You have failed to show the value of your widget/idea/service over your competitor(s)...

AND you have perhaps simply failed to have the backbone to say, "This is how much it costs."

Case In Point: The Big Green Egg Grill

The company that makes this thing is not a client of mine, but they exhibit the qualities I look for and do my best to instill in my clients. Those qualities are commitments:

- To good marketing
- To having a premium product
- To charging a premium price
- To selling to a base of fanatical customers
- To using good info-marketing and direct marketing techniques to support said practices.

They sell barbecue grills for $1,000. That's not a typo.

In a world where you can buy a grill for $9 at the drug store, or $30 at Target, these guys sell grills for anywhere from $350 at the "cheap" end to more than $1,000 at the high end. And they have plenty of add-ons and up-sells too!

It is worth studying and thinking about how to use the same ideas, techniques and approaches in your business–no matter what you sell.

Despite what you may think...your business is not different. You could learn a lot from the Big Green Egg Grill guys.

32

How to Get Famous and Make More Money

Write an eBook. I know a lot of people will tell you "eBooks are dead." To paraphrase Rick Blaine from the film Casablanca, they are misinformed.

Jeff Bezos (founder of Amazon.com) told USA Today recently that he sees a future where eBook sales will "surpass paperback sales sometime in the next 9 to 12 months."

That alone ought to put the old "eBooks are dead" rumor to rest once and for all.

Why Write An eBook?

1. Authors get listened to. Because they're authors, that's why.
2. Your idea has more perceived value if it's in an eBook than a "mere" blog post or article.
3. eBooks are easy for people to spread — which makes your idea easy to spread.

About 10 years ago, Seth Godin made an indelible impression on the web by writing an eBook and giving it away. His premise was that free ideas spread faster than expensive ones. He was (and still is) right.

Seth eventually created the site 'ChangeThis' as a platform for eBook authors. You don't have to use his platform. You can do this all on your own (if you want to).

Here are the steps to write your eBook

1. Make sure you know how NOT to write a book.
2. Finish your book.
3. Give away as many copies as you can.
4. Find ways to encourage others to share it. (One way is to ask them: "Please share this with as many people as you can.")

Now. Get to work.

33

The Simple "4-Legged Stool" of Internet Marketing

I've already hinted at this. But let me spell it out very clearly. When you get right down to it, this business is so simple it's almost funny.

To sell stuff online here's all you have to do... think of these as four legs of a stool. Without one of the legs, the stool is wobbly and unreliable. But with all four legs, your business can not just survive... but actually THRIVE.

ONE: Market Finding

The first leg of the stool is to simply find a market where people are unusually passionate and where they already spend a lot of money. Then you look into what they are actually buying. Identify the top products and see what their commonalities are. Also look for the unique features of each of top products.

TWO: Product Creation

Next combine the common elements and compile all the unique ones. Then create a product that includes all these things plus your own new ideas.

Now you have a product that is slightly better than the other products at the top of the market.

There are simple and easy ways to create the product yourself. And there are cheap, quick ways to have someone else do it, if that's what you prefer.

THREE: Traffic Getting

Next, you need to get your product seen by the people who will be interested in it. You can do this by recruiting some affiliates (this is not that hard to do), by using Pay Per Click ads through Google, buying cheap but effective banner ads, and any one of a dozen other strategies and tactics. It's NOT HARD. It just takes a LITTLE time & effort.

FOUR: Conversion

Finally you need to be able to turn those visitors into buyers. This comes down to good copywriting. There are some good books on the subject, and there are some great courses available (for instance I sell one of each: a book and course). You can even buy templates where you just fill in the blanks.

Then you test what works. Simple.

With those "four legs" under you, and the determination that you simply won't quit until you succeed, you'll do fine!

34

Shut Off Your Laptop, Boost Creativity

Creativity doesn't usually occur while you're screen-sucking.

To boost your number of creative ideas, you might consider getting away from your computer and introducing your brain to some new stimuli every now and then.

7 ways that work for me:

1. Enjoy coffee at a cafe (without iPhone, iPad, or laptop).
2. Take a walk outside.
3. Play ball with my dogs.
4. Listen to music.
5. Read fiction.
6. Talk with another human about Stuff That Matters.
7. Take a nap.

Those are some of my ways of boosting creativity. You will have your own. Just try to do something that doesn't involve the Internet.

To quote John Cleese: "We don't know where we get our ideas from. We do know that we do not get them from our laptops."

35

7 Surefire Ways to Make More Sales This Week

Here are seven surefire ways to make more sales this week:

1. Make more calls.
2. Talk to more customers.
3. Ask for the order more often.
4. Run more ads.
5. Hand out more business cards.
6. Call more passed customers.
7. Ask for more referrals.

I know, I know. Nothing new. That's the point. Stop looking for something new, and get to work.

36

Grow an A+ Marketing Brain

Here's a foolproof method to get yourself an A+ marketing brain, without having to pay for an expensive education.

Finish at least one good marketing book every week.

If you're not currently an avid reader, this might seem like a big deal. It's really not very difficult. Many marketing books are short, to begin with. And nobody said you have to read words printed on the page.

Audio books count. Most audio players have an option to speed up the audio -meaning you can often finish a book in half the time it might normally take.

If you read one good marketing book per week, you will have read 52 of them at the end of the year. How many of your peers do you think do that? How many of your competitors? Exactly. A+.

37

3 Quick Ways to Improve Your Writing

Want to improve your writing as quickly as possible? Here are the 3 best ways I know to do it.

1. Write every day.

Writing is like any skill; it improves only with practice. The more you write, the better your chances of improvement.

2. Re-write.

Put your writing away for a day or two and come back to it. You'll find ways to improve it. I know, it doesn't sound sexy–but it's still true.

3. Read every day.

Good writers are readers first and foremost. Reading well-written material is instructive in itself, and moreso if you're reading not only for content but also for the purpose of observing the craftsmanship.

If you say you don't have time to read, you're kidding yourself about wanting to be a better writer.

38

How to Write a Blog Post Every Day

I talk to a lot of people about blogging. One of the most common questions I get is, "Ray, how do you manage to write a blog post every single day?"

It's a good question. I believe that writing frequently and consistently is key to your blogging success. A few months ago I committed to writing daily as an experiment, to see what the practice would yield. I won't share the detailed results here, but I will say it has been well worth the effort, and I plan to continue.

Here are my best tips on how to manage writing a blog post every day:

Write in Batches

It's rare for me to write a single blog post at a time. Instead, I schedule a block of time (usually an hour or more), and write several blog posts in a row. This may not work for everyone, but it works for me. Once I'm in the flow of writing, it's better for me to keep on writing.

Write Shorter Posts

The best reason for writing shorter posts is very straightforward: people read them.

I've carefully observed the activity on this blog and noted that when I write longer posts I get fewer reactions. I know for certain that my readers prefer it when I write shorter posts. This has the advantage of allowing me to write more of them, making it easier to write something every day.

Keep a List of Possible Titles

I have a text file on my desktop that contains nothing but blog post title ideas. I get these ideas from a variety of sources: magazine covers, book titles, intriguing phrases I encounter when I'm reading, questions that I get via email or from my blog and other blogs I read. I capture these ideas when I'm on the go by entering them into Omnifocus on my iPhone, which automatically synchronizes with my MacBook Pro. Having this list of titles makes it easy to write when those scheduled blocks of writing time come up on my calendar. I'm never sitting at the keyboard wondering, "What shall I write about?"

Stay One Week Ahead

While I am not perfect at this, I do my best to stay a full week ahead in my post writing. This gives me the advantage of being able to write something topical if I want, but never being "squeezed" by deadlines. At times, I'm as much as 14 days ahead of schedule. This relieves a great deal of stress in my writing life.

Those are a few of the tips that allow me to produce a blog post every day.

39

3 Ways to Get New Clients... Today

Like so many things in life, getting new clients is not nearly as complicated as we sometimes like to make it.

Here are three ways you can get new clients (whether you're a freelancer, a consultant, or a salesperson) and get them today.

1. Call previous clients and ask for business.

I know. Seems simple when I say it, doesn't it?

2. Answer your email.

I mean, really answer it. Look for opportunities to help people with questions they didn't even realize they were asking.

Usually, it's easy to identify what problems people are having if you just pay attention to what they're actually saying.

Look through your inbox again, looking for opportunities to serve; these often lead to opportunities to get paid.

3. Call people in your network.

Pick up the phone, call people you know, and simply tell them:

87

"I'm looking for business. Do you know anybody I might be able to help with my services?"

Nothing glamorous here: just good, old-fashioned, uncompromising hard work gets the job done.

40

5 Essential Skills for Freelance Writers

There probably is not a comprehensive list of "perfect skills" every freelance copywriter should have, but here are five I feel need to be in every copywriter's toolkit.

Surprisingly, none of them are about writing copy.

Let's assume for the moment that you already know how to do that (please, if you say you're a copywriter, please tell me you know how to write copy).

Five essentials that will keep you happy, healthy, and wealthy:

1. The ability to understand other people and empathize with them.
2. Face-to-face selling skills.
3. The ability to shrug off rejection and criticism.
4. Discipline that enables you to sit down and actually do the work (lack of this skill is more common than you might think).
5. The ability to set realistic goals that stretch you and then to employ pigheaded discipline in the achievement of those goals.

If you possess these five skills, you're way ahead of most other writers in the race.

In fact, these five skills (along with your craft) can get you pretty much anything you need. You can get whatever you need to be successful, either through instruction or by hiring someone else.

41

3 Ways to Write Better Copy Faster

One of the keys to making more money as a freelance copywriter is being able to write good copy quickly.

The faster you write, the more you can write. The more you can write, the more money you can make.

Three tips on how to write copy faster (and probably better, too):

1. Work from an Outline

If you're a copywriter who's earned your stripes, you already have an intuitive sense of the structure of good sales copy (different structure for different media or formats, of course, but always a basic structure for each).

It's a good idea to have an outline available to use as a template (in Microsoft Word, for instance). Save yourself the mental effort of having to create the structure from scratch each time.

Organize your notes, clippings, and bits of copy within the outline. That way when you're ready to start writing, all your preliminary scribblings are at least in the right order.

2. Speak, Don't Type

As long as you aren't experiencing physiological or neurological problems, you speak much faster than you type.

If you're working from an outline (as suggested above) you should be able to dictate your copy at an incredibly rapid pace. You can either use software, such as DragonDictate, or pay to have a human being transcribe your copy.

Either way, it'll be much faster and more efficient, unless you're like my friend Michel Fortin, who has supernatural typing ability.

3. Build Up a Bank of "Copy Chunks"

Chances are, if you do much writing for clients, you end up writing very similar opens, guarantees, closing segments, and so forth.

Why not start collecting those "chunks" of copy, so you can simply cut and paste them into your first draft?

This technique alone can save you many hours of laborious and needlessly repetitive work.

Here's to speedier copy for you.

42

Relentless Rules That Make
Cash Registers Ring

Don't do any marketing or advertising that doesn't make money for your business; that doesn't make the cash register ring.

Here's the bad news: "brand building" is a door that is pretty much closed to the small- to medium- size company.

In today's over-communicated, oversaturated marketplace, the sheer mass required to achieve brand awareness is quite simply out of financial reach for all but the biggest companies. One could argue that such strategies don't always make sense for big companies either.

Here's what does not fail: holding your advertising and marketing accountable for its own results.

It doesn't take a rocket scientist to understand direct response marketing.

In fact, the steps are simple:

1. Launch a marketing or advertising campaign that you can measure.

Examples: phone calls completed, postcards returned, emails collected, sales made, etc.

2. Observe whether this campaign results in actual dollars coming in the door.

Did it generate sales?

3. If the answer to number two is "yes," repeat the process as needed.

If the answer is "no," if dollars do not flow in the door, try something else!

Is this a bit oversimplified? Yes, but not much. In fact, if you were to just follow this "oversimplified" formula to the letter, you would still be a lot better off than most businesses in America.

Make this promise to yourself:

"I will not engage in any marketing or advertising activity unless the results of said marketing or advertising activity can be objectively measured."

Then follow through on that promise. This alone will bring you more profits.

43

Resist Your Enemy

You have an enemy. Call it Chaos. Call it the Un-maker.
Call it Satan.

Your enemy is opposed to every act of creation on your part:
every act of kindness, generosity, beauty, and grace.

Your enemy wants you to think small, play it safe, and keep your
head down. Your enemy tries to tell you that an act of kindness
makes you weak. That forgiveness makes you a doormat.

Your enemy whispers in your ear when you have that idea for
a new product that would make people's lives better, and he says,
"That will never work... nobody will buy that... what a stupid idea...
it's too hard."

You know the enemy's voice well. If you're like 7 billion other
people on this planet, you have heeded it too often.

What if you just stopped listening? What if you told your enemy
to sit down and shut up? What if, today, you did something bold,
beautiful, crazy-cool?

Resist the enemy, and he will flee. He only ever had the power
you gave him by listening. Stop listening, and he is undone. The
world will look different to you.

Possibility unfurls. Miracle follows miracle. Try it. You'll like it.

44

What Does It Cost Not to Buy?

Here's a big secret that makes it easy to sell more of whatever you sell…

**Communicate what it will cost your
prospects if they don't buy from you**

What will it cost them in time, money, and effort if they don't solve their problem using your solution?

Just communicate clearly the cost of not buying from you today, and no "selling tricks" will be required.

What's that you say? You're not sure what it will cost them or even if it will cost them anything at all?

If that's the case, your problem is not a selling problem.

It's either a value problem or a value clarification problem.

Either way, you now know what to do next.

45

Say Yes, Get Paid More

I am a strong advocate for creating good boundaries in your business, and it holds especially true for freelance copywriters.

Training your customers on how to do business with you so that you can maximize your productivity and profits is vital.

I don't like to be the guy who always says "no." I like to find ways to say yes. For example, I don't haggle over my rates as a freelance copywriter and marketing consultant.

Does that mean that when I am in conversation with new clients, I'm quick to quote an astronomical rate, and turn them away if they suggest a lower payment? No, not at all.

I simply look for ways to change the nature of the offer, so that I'm able to accommodate their rate request.

It's as simple as asking a few targeted questions:

1. "If we were able to lower the price to what you ask, would you be ready to do business today?"

If the answer to this question is no, the discussion is really over isn't it?

2. "What part of the project seems most important to you, if we were able to deliver it for the price you suggest?"

This helps identify pieces of the project you may be able to eliminate, thus also eliminating the expense created by that particular activity, giving you more flexibility in your rate.

3. "What makes you think our service is only worth the amount you mentioned?"

You have to be careful of your tone of voice when asking this question; you don't want to sound confrontational.

But the issue may simply be one of perception of value. If the client doesn't feel that having me consult on a product launch is worth $50,000 upfront, no amount of sales technique will get him to write me that check. I need to determine where he feels the value is.

While these suggestions may not turn every price negotiation into a business deal, they will help you find ways to say yes to proposals you might've said no to in the past, and that can dramatically increase your bottom line.

46

3 Habits of Successful Freelance Copywriters

Interestingly, there are three habits that are shared by every successful freelance copywriter I know.

1: A Love of the Craft

Successful freelance copywriters simply love writing. They love doing it. And they love reading the work of others who love doing it.

Make no mistake: we are making ads, but we are also making art.

2: Discipline

Get rid of the preconception that copywriters are irresponsible, disheveled, professorial types.

The successful copywriter is a creature of sometimes frightening single-minded focus. That's why clients who find such a creature become loyal for life.

3: Discontent

While this might not be a great personal quality, successful freelance copywriters are never satisfied with their work.

Yes, they deliver on time, and they deliver excellent output but they are forever obsessing over how to make the copy better; how to improve the conversion rate, and how to beat the control.

In my book, that kind of self-motivation and positive discontent is a good quality when it comes to business.

If you are a person or a company who hires copywriters, look for these qualities.

If you are a copywriter who wants to be hired, look in the mirror.

Possession of these three qualities will make you a happy, healthy, and wealthy writer.

47

What It Takes to Succeed as a Freelance Copywriter

What does it take to succeed as a freelance copywriter? Well, I suppose it should go without saying that the first requirement is the ability to write good copy.

That detail out of the way, here are some qualities that are less common among copywriters but of equal importance.

The ability to treat your service like a business

Too many copywriters are woefully ignorant of the realities of running a business. A copywriting practice is a business, just like a law practice or any other professional service provider.

If you are playing the role of the "temperamental artist as copywriter," it probably means you're a dreadful businessperson. Your clients (almost all of them skilled entrepreneurs) hold that sort of mentality in great disdain.

Want more respect as a copywriter? Start acting like a businessperson.

The commitment to meet deadlines

Clients expect you to do what you said you were going to do, and they expect you to do it on the schedule you agreed to.

There are no excuses. I have never missed a deadline. I have, on occasion, renegotiated a deadline, but always ahead of time.

Repeat after me: "Deadlines are sacred. I shall not break them."

The skin of a rhinoceros

Look, I understand: writing is hard, and taking criticism is harder. Clients pay you to write and they have an expectation that their input will be accepted by you. After all, they're paying for the end product. They are going to be critical of what you write. You're writing about their baby–their business.

You've got to be able to smile when your clients are offering constructive criticism, even when they're wrong. You must be able to handle such situations with grace.

A crucial skill for you: the ability to subtly persuade clients that your way is the correct way.

Even more difficult, you've got to be able swallow your pride when your client has a good point... such as a point about some weakness in your copy (which is accurate more often than most copywriters would like to admit).

These skills are more difficult to develop than the skills of actually writing copy–at least for most copywriters. Most copywriters tend to be more right-brained and creative instead of left-brained and logical. I was gifted with a weird 50-50 combination of "artist/businessman" genetics.

I understand that not everyone was so fortunate.

Being conscious of the need for the skills I've outlined in this book, and becoming diligent in the development of these skills, will make you a much happier (and much richer) copywriter.

48

Simple Tricks Top Copywriters Use to Sell More

Writing persuasive copy is simple–but not always easy. The most persuasive techniques usually are the ones that are simplest.

Here are three simple tricks the top copywriters know and that help them sell more of whatever they're selling.

Know your prospects

This means doing your homework and knowing the audience you're writing to (and selling to) inside out.

You must know, at the very least their FFA's (fears, frustrations, and aspirations). If you know those three things, you have some powerful 'mojo' at your disposal.

Speak the language of your audience

If you are writing to golfers, for instance, you absolutely must not call the instruments of play anything other than clubs. Referring to "ball striking sticks" will earn your copy a quick trip to the trashcan.

I know the example is ridiculous, but I see copywriters making mistakes equally as ridiculous all the time.

Know your product

Again, a seemingly obvious point, yet one of the most frequently violated principles of writing persuasive copy.

The more you know about your product, the more persuasively you will be able to communicate about it.

Newbie copywriters would do well to study the greats, particularly Eugene Schwartz, who often read a book four (or more) times, and had 100 pages of notes written in his own hand, when he finally sat down to write the copy that would sell the book.

As I said, simple–not necessarily easy.

49

5 Good Reasons to Blog

Many business owners, freelancers, and solo professionals wonder; "Should I have a blog? Is it worth the effort? What does a blog do for me?"

My answer: yes, you need a blog. And here are 5 good reasons why:

1: It's good for business

When I started blogging, it didn't take long for me to realize blogging was building my business. I get a steady flow of new business from people who say something like, "Well, I started reading your blog and finally decided I would call you."

2: Self-expression

Once upon a time, I was a radio DJ. I was highly-rated, successful, and loving it. Being on the radio was my own personal megaphone. It was my way of being heard.

Now I get that same satisfaction from blogging. You can too. Now everyone's a DJ!

3: Building a relationship with my readers

There's nothing like a blog to build a relationship with your readers. My blog is the source of most of the conversations I have with my readers.

4: Marketing

I know there are many who say you can't "monetize" a blog. Really? My own blog has brought me... well, let's call it "a substantial amount" of revenue. And I don't even use Adsense (as of this writing).

One of the very best Internet marketers is a guy name Dave Winer. You'd never categorize him as a marketer, but he is a consummate marketer, although most of his readers probably don't realize it.

5: Research and testing

The quickest way I know to test a new idea, get some feedback, or get an answer is... make a post on your blog about the new idea. Those are just 5 reasons–there are dozens more.

50

Don't Interrupt Me

Interruptions cost you dearly.

As a writer, I know that allowing myself to be interrupted by a client or vendor ("Hey Ray–got a minute to talk about the new logo?") can seem harmless... but it isn't.

That interruption costs me (a) the state of "flow" I was in while working, maybe impossible to recover, (b) the time of the interruption itself, and (c) the time it takes me to get back into the "zone" with what I was working on... minimum 20 minutes, maybe longer.

I can't afford to let that happen. Especially not in the "New Economy." My clients and customers can't afford for me to let that happen.

I once had a client who loved to call me at 11pm at night and talk for two hours. I tried to tell him I worked set hours and was available at those times, but he didn't seem to understand. When our first project was finished, I fired him. His dysfunction did not automatically become my problem.

Be warned–people will waste your time, if you let them.

Will you let them? Be polite, be loving... but don't be a victim. In the end, if you guard your time, you are being most respectful of other people.

Think about it: if you allow yourself to be interrupted, or your time to be wasted when you should have been doing something else... who suffers? Your clients. Your customers. Your family ("Sorry honey, I have to stay late because I wasted 2 hours today listening to the web team make excuses...").

You're not serving anyone by being a poor steward of your time.

51

Your 10 Day Challenge

You've reached the end of the book, and now you have a choice. The choice between two roads.

The road on your left is the one most people will take. It is the road of least resistance. It is the seductive road of the familiar, the routine, the habitual. Doing the same old things you've always done. The problem with this road is it leads to the same results you've always experienced.

The road on your right is the road not chosen by most. That's because it's unfamiliar, contains the unknown, the possibility of danger, or difficulty, or simply of getting lost. The road on the right is where the risk is. But here's something I know about you…

If you picked up this book and read this far, you're the kind of person who takes the road on the right. You are an entrepreneur. You inherently are drawn to risk, and the rewards that lay on the other side of it.

If you want to take the road on the right, this book can make a true impact in your life and in your business. I propose a 10 day challenge…

Each day, for the next 10 days, pick one idea from the book and implement that idea with the full intention of your will. Notice the results you are getting. If you will take this 10 day challenge, you're always free to return to the more comfortable road afterwards, if you want.

My guess is you will not do that. 0Because you're the kind of person who chooses the right road.

Ray Edwards
Spokane, Washington

How to Contact Ray

If you are interested in online business, marketing, copywriting, and how to be a follower of Jesus in the marketplace, Ray can help. For more information about keynotes and workshops, contact Ray Edwards International, Inc.:

Phone: (509) 624–2220
Email: info@RayEdwards.com
Online: www.RayEdwards.com

Ray Edwards International, Inc
2910 E 57th AveSte 5 #330
Spokane, WA 99223

Sign-up for Ray Edwards' email newsletter at:

www.RayEdwards.com

To purchase bulk copies of this book at a discount for your customers, or for your organization, please contact Ray Edward's international, Inc.:

specialsales@RayEdwards.com or (509) 624–2220

7753206R00076

Printed in Great Britain
by Amazon.co.uk, Ltd.,
Marston Gate.